Rising Strong
Building Positive
High Self-Esteem
for a Fulfilling Life

A Practical Guide for Students, Employees, Leaders & Entrepreneurs

Gerard Assey

Rising Strong: Building Positive High Self-Esteem for a Fulfilling Life

A Practical Guide for Students, Employees, Leaders & Entrepreneurs

By

Gerard Assey

Published by:
Gerard Assey
19/18, Palli Arasan Street
Anna Nagar East
Chennai - 600 102

ISBN: 978-81-989262-8-9

(Cover: Courtesy: JComp-Freepik @www.Freepik.com)

Table of Contents

Disclaimer:

Any resemblance (names, characters, and scenarios used in this book, including testimonies and personal stories) to actual persons, living or dead, or actual events is purely coincidental. These examples are used solely for illustrative and teaching purposes.
The intent is to inspire and equip readers, not to depict real individuals or specific events. No harm or misrepresentation is intended.

Preface

Why This Book Was Written

There's a silent epidemic affecting millions across the world — not a disease of the body, but of the soul. It creeps in quietly and robs people of their potential, relationships, happiness, and impact. It doesn't always scream for attention, yet it whispers lies that become life sentences: *"I'm not good enough." "I don't matter." "Why would anyone listen to me?"* These aren't just passing thoughts. They are the roots of low self-esteem, and they grow deep — often invisible to others, but painfully real to those who live with them every single day.

I've met these people — in classrooms, offices, boardrooms, church pews, coffee shops, and late-night conversations. I've coached a promising student who couldn't look up while speaking because he didn't think his voice deserved to be heard. I've watched talented employees crumble under the weight of one harsh comment from a boss. I've seen middle-aged entrepreneurs self-sabotage the very business they started because deep down, they didn't believe they were worthy of success.

And I've lived some of that story myself.

This book was born from a burden — a deep desire to speak directly to those who are stuck. Not because they lack skill or opportunity, but because they've internalized a story that says they're not enough. I wanted to write something real — not academic or sterile — but raw, honest, and deeply practical. A book that you won't just read, but use. A book you can come back to when the voices in your head get loud again.

Low self-esteem is not a personality flaw — it is a learned belief system. And what's learned can be unlearned. More than motivation, you need a method. More than theory, you need tools. More than stories, you need steps forward. That's what this book is about.

I want to invite you on a journey — not to become someone else, but to finally recognize the worth of who you've always been.

Who This Book Is For

This book is for you if:

- ✓ You've ever held back in life, not because you lacked capability, but because you questioned your worth.
- ✓ You walk into rooms and immediately shrink, convinced others are more qualified, more likable, more deserving.
- ✓ You are a student, employee, manager, or entrepreneur constantly battling imposter syndrome, even though others see potential in you.
- ✓ You constantly seek approval, but still feel like a fraud inside.
- ✓ You keep saying yes to people while silently resenting it because you don't believe you have the right to say no.
- ✓ You're doing okay externally — job, family, titles — but internally, you feel small, unsure, and afraid to speak your truth.

Whether you're 18 or 58, this book is designed to meet you where you are. It's not just for people at rock bottom. It's for anyone who has settled for a version of themselves that is less than what they were created to be.

This is also for parents, teachers, mentors, and managers — those in positions to shape the self-esteem of others. If you work with people in any capacity, this book will help you build them up instead of breaking them down, whether intentionally or unknowingly.

This book does not require prior knowledge of psychology. It's not written in jargon or wrapped in academic theory. It's written in a language we all speak — the language of real life, real struggles, and real change.

How to Use This Book Effectively

Let me say this up front: This book won't work if it stays on your shelf or screen. You need to work it. And the more honestly and intentionally you do, the more powerfully it will transform your self-view — and in turn, your life.

Here's how to get the most out of this journey:

1. Read Slowly, Reflect Deeply

Each chapter ends with exercises, journaling prompts, and action plans. These are not optional extras — they are core to your growth. Take your time. Don't rush. Reflect honestly and write things down. The goal isn't speed. It's transformation.

2. Bring a Journal

Keep a physical or digital journal where you can write your responses, track your thoughts, and revisit your growth. Many sections will ask you to complete lists, write letters, or document your internal dialogue. Trust the process.

3. Use Real Names Where Possible

Wherever prompted, try to write about real people, real moments, and real feelings. The more personal and specific you are, the deeper the healing.

4. Return Often

Self-esteem isn't built once. It's maintained. You'll find that different chapters will speak more to you at different stages. Mark the pages that resonate. Create your own "go-to" pages for the tough days.

5. Share It Forward

If a story, insight, or exercise helps you, consider sharing it with someone else who may need it. Sometimes, in helping others rise, we rise higher ourselves.

Let me leave you with one true story before we begin.

Anita (name changed), a 29-year-old marketing executive, came to me during a career coaching session. *"I feel stuck,"* she said. *"I'm great at what I do. My team says I'm a natural leader. But every time I'm offered a promotion, I freeze. I hear this voice in my head saying, You're just pretending. One day they'll find out you're not as good as they think."*

She had been carrying that voice since she was 11 — when a schoolteacher publicly called *her "below average, written off and forgettable."* That day, a part of her shrunk. For 18 years, she did well on the outside, but that teacher's voice lived rent-free in her head.

It took time, but Anita began to confront the lie, rewrite the narrative, and eventually, own her worth. Today, she's not only leading her department — she's mentoring others in the same journey.

That same shift is available to you. This book will show you how.

Let's begin the process of rising strong — not as someone new, but as someone finally able to see the truth:

You were never lacking. You just stopped believing.
Welcome to your journey back to *you*.

Self-Esteem Assessment/Audit Form
"Where Do I Stand?"

Below is a **detailed, self-reflective Self-Esteem Assessment/Audit Form** titled ***"Where Do I Stand?"*** It is designed to help you get a clear, honest baseline of your current level of self-esteem before starting the journey through '*Rising Strong: Building Positive High Self-Esteem for a Fulfilling Life*'.

This comprehensive tool includes various dimensions—**emotional, cognitive, behavioral, relational, and situational**—and is scored to offer a clear picture of where you currently stand. It also includes a reflective scoring interpretation section and journaling prompts for deeper self-discovery.

Self-Esteem Assessment Audit

Title: "Where Do I Stand?" – *A Personal Self-Esteem Check-In*

Instructions: Read each statement carefully and rate how true it feels for you using the scale below.

Scale:

5 – Always True
4 – Often True
3 – Sometimes True
2 – Rarely True
1 – Never True

Section 1: Internal Beliefs & Self-Perception

Statement	Score (1-5)
I believe I have value just for being who I am, not based on what I do.	
I feel comfortable in my own skin.	
I talk to myself in a kind, encouraging way.	
I believe I deserve respect from others.	
I trust my decisions without excessive doubt or regret.	
I acknowledge my strengths without feeling arrogant.	
I can accept compliments without deflecting or downplaying them.	
I believe my opinions are valid even if others disagree.	

Section 2: Emotional & Behavioral Responses

Statement	Score (1-5)
I can handle criticism without taking it personally or shutting down.	
I don't constantly seek approval from others to feel okay about myself.	
I am able to say "no" without feeling guilty or fearful.	
I don't let past mistakes define my identity.	
I bounce back from failure or rejection with resilience.	
I don't feel the need to prove my worth through achievements.	

Statement	Score (1-5)
I celebrate my small wins and progress, not just big successes.	
I take care of myself physically, emotionally, and mentally.	

Section 3: Relationships & Boundaries

Statement	Score (1-5)
I don't stay in unhealthy relationships out of fear or unworthiness.	
I attract and choose people who value and respect me.	
I can express my needs clearly and assertively.	
I don't let others' moods or opinions determine how I feel about myself.	
I set and maintain healthy personal boundaries.	
I don't compare myself negatively to others all the time.	
I feel free to be myself around others without pretending or performing.	
I feel equal—not superior or inferior—to others in social settings.	

Section 4: Life Choices & Confidence

Statement	Score (1-5)
I pursue goals that matter to me, even if they scare me.	
I don't sabotage good opportunities because I feel unworthy of them.	
I believe I have something important to offer the world.	
I make decisions based on my values, not pressure or fear.	
I trust that failure is a learning process, not a verdict on my worth.	
I don't let fear of judgment stop me from speaking or acting.	
I feel a sense of direction and purpose in my life.	
I believe I can make a positive impact in the lives of others.	

Scoring Interpretation

Total Possible Score: 160

Add up your scores from all 32 questions.

Score Ranges:

128–160 –Strong Self-Esteem

You demonstrate a healthy, grounded sense of self-worth. You likely bounce back from setbacks, hold your space in relationships, and live with clarity and courage.

96–127 – **Emerging Self-Esteem**

You're on your way. There are positive foundations, but some self-doubt or fear may still be influencing your behavior and thoughts. This book will greatly support your ongoing growth.

64–95 – Vulnerable Self-Esteem

There are clear signs of self-esteem struggles that may be affecting your work, relationships, and identity. Healing is possible—and this book is here to walk you through it step-by-step

Below 64 – Critical Zone

You may be experiencing deep self-worth wounds rooted in past pain, trauma, or ongoing toxic influences. You're not alone—and it's never too late to rebuild. Take this journey seriously. Consider also reaching out for counseling, mentorship, or faith-based support as you read through this book.

Reflection Prompts:
(Optional but Highly Recommended)

After completing your score, reflect on the following in a journal or notebook:

- ✓ *Which three statements did you score the lowest on?*
- ✓ *Why do you think these areas are especially difficult for you?*
- ✓ *Which three statements did you score highest on?*
- ✓ *What helps you feel strong in those areas?*
- ✓ *Whose voice echoes in your mind when you feel "not enough"?*
- ✓ *What message from that person still affects you?*
- ✓ *What would your life look like if you believed, fully and truly, that you are worthy?*

Write freely. Let the vision lead you.

This audit can be repeated after finishing the book and again every 3-6 months to track progress.

Chapter 1: Understanding Self-Esteem The Foundation of a Fulfilling Life

What Is Self-Esteem?

Self-esteem is the quiet yet powerful belief we carry about our own value and worth. It's not just about what we *do*, but how we *see* ourselves—our identity, our significance, and our sense of being enough just as we are. It is that deep inner voice that whispers (or shouts) either "I matter" or "I don't."

Many people mistake self-esteem as something we only need to think about when we're in crisis. But the truth is, every single decision you make—from how you present yourself in a meeting, to how you deal with rejection, to how you love and allow yourself to be loved—is filtered through your level of self-esteem.

At its core, self-esteem answers two questions:

- ✓ *Do I believe I am worthy of love and respect?*
- ✓ *Do I believe I have the right to exist and take up space as I am?*

These aren't questions we consciously ask ourselves daily—but they drive our behaviors. The person who never speaks up in meetings. The student who doesn't raise their hand. The entrepreneur who undercharges for their work. All these are manifestations of how they unconsciously see themselves.

And it's not always loud. Sometimes, low self-esteem wears a smile. It's masked with busy schedules, endless achievements, or people-pleasing. But beneath it all is a painful belief: *I'm not enough.*

The Difference Between Confidence and Self-Esteem

It's easy to confuse confidence with self-esteem, but they're not the same.

Confidence is *external*. It's the belief that you can do something. You can be confident in public speaking, or your driving skills, or your ability to solve a math problem.

Self-esteem, on the other hand, is *internal*. It's your overall sense of self-worth, regardless of what you can or can't do. You might be incredibly skilled and admired by others, yet still feel deeply unworthy and undeserving on the inside.

Think of it like this:

Confidence says: *"I can do this presentation well."*

Self-esteem says: *"Even if I mess up this presentation, I'm still valuable and loved."*

That's why many outwardly "confident" people secretly struggle with self-esteem. Actors, CEOs, teachers, even therapists—people who seem self-assured—may still privately feel like frauds. Because while their competence may be celebrated, their *core identity* feels shaky.

High vs. Low Self-Esteem: A Quick Comparison

To understand what's at stake, imagine two people facing the same challenge—say, being passed over for a promotion.

Rakesh, who has high self-esteem, processes it as disappointment, but he doesn't let it define him. He thinks, *"It wasn't my time, maybe I can ask for feedback and grow from this."* He still sees himself as valuable and respected.

Priya, who has low self-esteem, spirals into self-doubt. Her mind tells her, *"I knew I wasn't good enough. They probably regret hiring me in the first place."* She begins to withdraw and second-guess even her small decisions.

Here's the crucial difference: It's not the event, but the interpretation of the event that reveals the level of self-esteem.

- ✓ High self-esteem isn't arrogance. It doesn't say, *"I'm better than others."* It says, *"I'm no less than others."* It's grounded, stable, and not easily shaken by success or failure. It allows a person to admit mistakes without crumbling, and to celebrate wins without needing validation.
- ✓ Low self-esteem, on the other hand, is unstable. It makes you swing between extremes—overachieving to prove your worth, or giving up because you believe you're worthless. Either way, you are living in reaction to a core lie: *You are not enough.*

Debunking Myths About Self-Esteem

Myth 1: People with high self-esteem are loud and assertive.

Not true. Some of the most grounded people have a quiet confidence that doesn't seek the spotlight. They are comfortable in their skin without needing attention.

Myth 2: Self-esteem is fixed—you either have it or you don't.

False. Self-esteem is *learned*. And what's learned can be *unlearned* and rebuilt. Just like physical fitness, emotional strength can be developed over time with consistent effort.

Myth 3: High self-esteem means you always feel good about yourself.
Not at all. Everyone has bad days and insecurities. But people with high self-esteem know how to separate feelings from facts. They may feel low, but they don't define themselves by the low moment.
Myth 4: It's selfish to focus on self-esteem.
That's the biggest lie of all. Low self-esteem is what often leads to selfish behaviors—neediness, manipulation, insecurity-driven decisions. Healthy self-esteem actually helps you *love and serve others better* because you are not operating from a place of lack.

Real-Life Snapshot: Rina's Battle With Her Inner Critic
Rina was 33, a team lead at a growing tech company, and on paper, her life looked great. She had a good salary, a great team, and a boss who supported her.
But Rina dreaded one thing: *performance reviews.* Every single time, even when they were positive, she would go into a spiral.
"I would scan every sentence for hidden criticism," she told me once in a coaching session. "Even if 95% was praise, I'd fixate on the 5% that said I could 'work on delegation.' My mind would immediately say, *'You're a failure. You're not really a leader.'"*
Rina had lived with a voice in her head that had taken root in childhood. Her father, a brilliant but emotionally distant man, only ever spoke to correct her mistakes. He believed he was pushing her toward excellence. But all it taught her was: *"I'm only good when I don't mess up."*

In the workplace, this internalized voice became her worst enemy. She couldn't receive compliments. She second-guessed every decision. She overworked, micromanaged her team, and avoided feedback.

Through our coaching, we began to unpack this voice. She started naming it—she called it "The Critic." Then, we brought in a new voice—"The Witness." This was her rational, kinder self that simply observed facts without judgment.

It wasn't magic. It was messy and slow. But today, Rina approaches her reviews with a new mindset. She still feels nervous, but she no longer lets The Critic drive the car. She listens. She reflects. And she grows—without shrinking.

Her esteem wasn't built by affirmations alone, but by challenging the old voices and choosing a new narrative—one where she was already enough, even before she achieved anything.

Action Plan: Laying the Groundwork for Your Esteem Journey

If you've read this far and something stirred in you—an old memory, a repeated struggle, or a lingering fear—it means this chapter has already started to do its work.

Let's make it practical.

Step 1: Journal Your Internal Script

Take 10 minutes and write down some of the most common thoughts you hear in your head about yourself. Be brutally honest. Don't censor it.

Then ask:

- ✓ Who first said this to me?
- ✓ Is this voice telling the truth—or just repeating something I internalized?

- ✓ What would I say to a friend who believed this about themselves?

Step 2: Craft a Self-Statement

Now, write a single sentence that you want to *begin* to believe. Not a wild affirmation, but something truthful and gentle.

Examples:

- ✓ "I am learning to see myself as valuable, even when I feel otherwise."
- ✓ "I can make mistakes and still be worthy of love and respect."

Write this down. Keep it where you can see it.

Step 3: Watch for the Critic

Over the next few days, become aware of your inner voice. Each time you catch your Critic speaking, mentally say: *"Thank you, but I'm choosing a different story now."* Replace it with your self-statement.

You don't have to have it all figured out today. But today, you took the first and most important step: You looked at the truth of how you see yourself. That takes courage.

The rest of this book will help you *rebuild what life, people, and fear tried to break down*. And it begins here — with the choice to rise.

Let's move forward.

Chapter 2: Root Causes of Low Self-Esteem

You weren't born doubting yourself.

Watch a child who hasn't yet been shamed by the world. They laugh loudly. They run without worrying if they look silly. They ask for what they want. They believe they are worthy of love and attention. Self-esteem is natural at birth — but something happens along the way.

This chapter is about that "something." We don't wake up one day thinking we're not enough. We are taught to feel that way. Not always intentionally, not always through words. But through consistent, shaping experiences that slowly carve our self-perception.

To rebuild self-esteem, we must understand where the cracks began. Let's go there together.

Childhood Conditioning: Parents, Caregivers, and Early Messages

The first voices that shape us are the ones we hear at home. Parents and caregivers may not realize it, but they are the architects of a child's early self-worth.

When love is conditional — based on grades, behavior, or performance — the child learns a dangerous lesson: *I must earn love.*

When mistakes are met with shame instead of correction, the child learns: *I am bad, not just what I did.*

Even well-meaning parents can unintentionally plant seeds of inadequacy. A father who says, *"You're just like your lazy uncle,"* may forget the comment — but the child won't. A mother who compares her children — *"Why can't you be more like your sister?"* — may think she's motivating, but she's unknowingly wounding.

I once met a 40-year-old woman, Anjali, who still flinched when people raised their voices. As a child, she was often yelled at for crying too much. Her emotions were labeled as *"too much," "too dramatic," "a problem."* So she grew up suppressing them. Even as an adult, she didn't trust herself. She'd second-guess every feeling, every response. *"Maybe I'm overreacting,"* she'd say, even when she was clearly mistreated.

Low self-esteem often doesn't begin with loud abuse. It begins with small, repeated messages that tell a child: *You are not okay as you are.*

The Role of Teachers and the Education System

The classroom is another battlefield for esteem.

Teachers carry immense influence — sometimes more than they realize. A single comment can become a defining voice in a child's life.

Take Rakesh, for example. At 12, he was slow in math but loved storytelling. One day, when he read his story out loud, his teacher laughed and said, *"Well, at least you're good at something… you'll need it, since math clearly won't feed you."*

The class laughed. Rakesh laughed too. But something broke.

Years later, he was working in marketing — a field that thrives on storytelling — yet he still felt like he wasn't *"smart enough."* He wouldn't apply for leadership roles, always fearing he'd be *"found out."* He didn't even know where that fear came from — until he revisited that classroom memory.

We often forget that children are always listening, and they tend to believe what adults tell them. Not just through words, but tone, comparison, and treatment.

An education system that over-values scores and under-values identity quietly tells children: *You are your marks. You are your rank. You are your failure if you fall behind.*

That message sticks, long after report cards are thrown away.

Negative Authority Figures: Bosses and Mentors

Fast forward to adulthood. Now you're in the workplace. You've grown, you've learned… and yet, the old voices find new faces.

Bosses, managers, and even mentors often become the next powerful voices in shaping esteem. A harsh boss who ridicules you publicly, a manager who micromanages everything you do, a mentor who constantly reminds you how far you have to go — all these can resurrect those same childhood wounds.

Vikas was a graphic designer, brilliant but anxious. His first boss, in his first job, never said a kind word. *"Is this all you could come up with?"* was her standard feedback. Once, she told him in front of the whole team, *"If I wanted basic designs, I'd use a free app."*

Even after changing jobs, Vikas couldn't shake the fear of being evaluated. He'd present his work with disclaimers: *"I'm not sure if this is good,"* or "*You can totally reject it."* His esteem had been worn down by someone who should have built it up.

Sadly, toxic bosses are common. But even in the absence of toxicity, a lack of affirmation or guidance can cause damage. Silence can feel like disapproval.

When you never hear *"you did well,"* you start assuming you didn't.

Cultural and Societal Conditioning

Let's talk about society's role.

In some cultures, humility is overemphasized to the point of invisibility. Children are told, *"Don't talk too much," "Don't boast," "Stay humble."* While humility is a virtue, when misapplied, it becomes shame. The child learns, *"If I shine too much, I'll be punished."* So they hide.

In other cultures, success is narrowly defined: stable job, marriage by 30, house, car, children. If you take a different path, you're seen as a failure. Even if you're happy.

This can be especially hard on creatives, late bloomers, women choosing career over marriage (or vice versa), or anyone who doesn't fit the "script."

Ravi, an independent filmmaker, once told me, *"My parents still introduce me as 'the one who's trying to do something in film.'"* Even with awards under his belt, he felt like a disappointment. Why? Because his job didn't fit the mold.

Society shapes esteem subtly, through expectations, roles, and collective opinions. You begin to think: *If I don't meet the standard, I must be substandard.*

Media and Unrealistic Standards

And then there's the ever-present voice of media.

We live in a world of curated lives — filtered photos, success reels, lifestyle influencers. Every scroll through social media quietly whispers: *You're not doing enough. You don't look good enough. You're behind.*

When we fear both failing and succeeding, we stay stuck — never falling, never flying.

Relationship Issues and Dependency

Low self-esteem often shows up in relationships — not through neediness alone, but through *who* we choose, and *how* we behave in those connections.

People with low self-worth often:

- ✓ Stay in toxic or one-sided relationships because they don't believe they deserve better.
- ✓ Avoid conflict completely, fearing rejection or abandonment.
- ✓ Lose their identity trying to keep others happy.
- ✓ Confuse love with validation — needing constant reassurance to feel secure.

This emotional dependency isn't always dramatic. Sometimes, it's in subtle patterns: not voicing your needs, accepting disrespect, or staying quiet to avoid "being too much."

Priya, a schoolteacher, once told me, *"In all my relationships, I gave more than I got. And I called that love."* But over time, she realized it wasn't love — it was fear of being alone. It was the belief that if she stopped trying so hard, she'd be left behind.

Low self-esteem tells us we are only as worthy as others' approval. And so we become addicted to affection, chasing love as if it were proof of our value.

Underperformance at Work or School

Not everyone with low self-esteem underperforms. Some overwork to prove themselves. But many slowly sabotage their own growth, believing — consciously or unconsciously — that they can't, or shouldn't, succeed.

This might show up as:

- ✓ Not applying for promotions even when qualified.
- ✓ Avoiding leadership roles.
- ✓ Settling for average grades despite higher potential.
- ✓ Downplaying accomplishments *("It was nothing," "Anyone could have done it.")*

A college student named Karan once told me, *"I don't even try hard anymore. What's the point? I'll never be as good as the others."* He had internalized a belief that effort wouldn't matter, so he stopped showing up fully — not because he didn't care, but because he didn't think he was *allowed* to thrive.

Low self-esteem makes you play small. It keeps you in the shadows — not because the spotlight isn't available, but because you've convinced yourself you don't belong there.

Addiction to Approval and Perfectionism

This is one of the most deceptive signs. Perfectionism often looks like high standards and discipline. But underneath it lies a fragile core: *If I am not perfect, I am not enough.*

People with low self-esteem often seek approval through performance. They become perfectionists — trying to avoid criticism by being flawless. They constantly seek validation from bosses, parents, partners, or social media. They thrive on praise, but collapse when they don't receive it.

Kavitha, a senior HR manager, was known for her excellence. But it came at a cost. She slept four hours a night, rewrote reports five times, and never celebrated her wins. *"If I let my guard down,"* she

said, *"I'm afraid people will see I'm not as good as they think."*
Approval becomes oxygen. And without it, the person feels lost, anxious, and invisible.
Perfectionism is not a sign of strength — it's often a symptom of shame. It's the silent cry of someone trying desperately to earn what should have been theirs all along: the belief that *they are enough.*

Case Study: Meena's Pattern of Choosing the Wrong Relationships

Meena was in her early forties when she came for coaching. She had just ended her third relationship in seven years — all with men who treated her poorly, emotionally manipulated her, or simply withdrew without explanation.
"I don't understand," she said with tears in her eyes. *"I give everything. I love deeply. But I always end up being used or left."*
As we traced her story, a pattern emerged.
Growing up, Meena had been the emotional caretaker for her family. Her father was distant. Her mother was overwhelmed. She learned early on that her value came from being useful. From pleasing. From fixing.
So in adulthood, she was drawn to emotionally unavailable men. Men she could chase, please, and prove herself to. Each time she was abandoned, it reinforced the belief: *"I'm not enough to be chosen."*
We worked on reframing her story — not just intellectually, but emotionally. She started setting boundaries, speaking up for her needs, and slowly shifting her self-talk. Her healing didn't happen in one session, but in one decision at a time.

The next time she met someone who didn't treat her with value, she didn't chase. She let go. And for the first time, she said, *"I'm not broken. I'm just done settling."*

Self-Assessment Checklist: Is Low Self-Esteem Affecting You?

Take a moment to read through the following statements. If several feel true for you, it's a sign that your self-esteem may need healing.

- ✓ *I often feel like I'm not good enough, no matter what I do.*
- ✓ *I apologize often — even when I've done nothing wrong.*
- ✓ *I avoid speaking up for fear of sounding stupid or being judged.*
- ✓ *I stay in relationships that make me feel small or unimportant.*
- ✓ *I struggle to accept compliments or downplay my achievements.*
- ✓ *I fear failing — but also fear what might happen if I succeed.*
- ✓ *I constantly compare myself to others and feel behind.*
- ✓ *I depend heavily on praise or approval to feel good about myself.*
- ✓ *I feel anxious when I make mistakes or show vulnerability.*
- ✓ *I often push myself to be perfect to feel worthy or accepted.*

Don't worry if many of these resonate. Awareness is not defeat — it's the beginning of freedom.

This chapter has shown you how low self-esteem manifests — not just in how you think, but in how you live, love, work, and respond to the world.

But here's the good news: everything you've seen in this chapter is *changeable*. Every belief can be rewritten. Every habit can be reshaped. And every painful story can become the beginning of a stronger, truer one.

In the next chapter, we'll begin shifting gears. We'll look at the *benefits* of building high, healthy self-esteem — and why it's not just good for *you*, but for everyone you influence.

You're doing the inner work that most people avoid. And that, in itself, is a sign of strength.

Shall we keep going?

Chapter 5: The Turning Point – Why You Must Decide to Rise

There comes a moment in every journey of healing when looking back becomes more painful than moving forward. A moment when the familiar weight of staying small finally outweighs the fear of stepping into the unknown.

This is the turning point.

No book, no teacher, no coach — not even the deepest pain — can force someone to change unless they decide. That moment of decision, where a person says, *"Enough is enough. I refuse to live like this any longer"* — that's when transformation truly begins.

This chapter is about that moment. About what happens when you stop surviving and start choosing. About what opens up when you begin to believe you were never meant to stay small.

The Cost of Staying Small

It's easy to downplay the cost of low self-esteem. After all, most people with low self-esteem still get through life. They hold jobs, raise families, smile for photos, post on social media.

But functioning isn't flourishing.

The real cost of low self-worth isn't always visible in external failures — it's in the opportunities never taken, the dreams quietly buried, and the relationships lived in fear instead of freedom.

The cost is:

- ✓ Years spent in roles you've outgrown because you don't believe you can do more.
- ✓ Avoiding love or settling for less, because you think that's all you deserve.
- ✓ A constant inner voice that says, *"Don't speak up, don't stand out, don't try too hard."*

Think about this: what have you *not done* because of your low self-esteem? What have you missed out on?

Tarun, a soft-spoken man in his mid-thirties, once told me during a workshop: *"For ten years, I've had a business idea. I've seen people with less experience and fewer resources do it. But every time I think about starting, something inside me says, 'Who do you think you are?' So I wait. I delay. I shrink."*

He paused and added, *"I think I'm more afraid of who I could be than who I am right now."*

Staying small feels safe — but it comes at a quiet, devastating cost: the loss of who you could have become.

The Link Between Esteem and Success

We often think success leads to self-esteem. But in truth, esteem fuels succe**ss** — not just in career, but in relationships, health, finances, and emotional well-being.

People with high self-esteem don't believe they're better than others — they simply believe they are *worth investing in*. They try. They take chances. They learn from failures instead of letting them define their identity.

Here's what high self-esteem looks like in action:

- ✓ Applying for the promotion even if you don't meet 100% of the criteria.

- ✓ Leaving a toxic relationship because you know you deserve peace.
- ✓ Starting the fitness journey not because you hate your body, but because you value it.
- ✓ Saying "no" without guilt and "yes" without apology.

This is not about arrogance or ego. It's about alignment — living in a way that reflects the truth that you are already valuable, not waiting for the world to validate you.

Real success — the kind that's sustainable and satisfying — starts with believing you're allowed to take up space, pursue your purpose, and ask for what you need.

Stories of Transformation: When Ordinary People Chose to Change

Every person who rises does so by first making a decision.

Let me share three snapshots of people — just like you — who decided they were done playing small.

1. Rita, the Homemaker Who Became a Community Leader

Rita spent 18 years caring for her family. Her children thrived, her husband built his career, but she felt invisible. She would often say, *"I'm just a housewife."* The word "just" became her identity.

Then one day, while attending a local health camp, she overheard someone say, *"These women don't understand anything."* That stung.

She didn't react. But she went home, looked in the mirror, and whispered to herself: *"You're not nothing."*

That week, she joined an adult learning program. Six months later, she volunteered to teach basic literacy to other women in her neighborhood. Today, Rita leads a network of 40 women who run awareness drives, health camps, and small savings groups.

Her self-esteem didn't come from applause — it came from action. She rose because she decided to.

2. Vinod, the Call Centre Agent Who Learned to Speak Up

Vinod had a stammer growing up. He was mocked in school, often called "mute genius" because he was bright but quiet. Even as an adult, the fear of public speaking haunted him.

But one day, after attending a client presentation where his teammate fumbled facts Vinod knew well, he realized: *I'm allowing fear to steal my voice.*

He signed up for a public speaking course. The first session, he barely spoke. But he kept showing up. By the fourth session, he gave a 3-minute talk on "The Power of Second Chances." His hands shook. His voice cracked. But he stood tall.

Within a year, Vinod was promoted to a trainer's role. Not because his speech was perfect — but because his *decision* was.

3. Saira, the Teen Who Refused to Be Defined by a Label

Saira was told all her life that she was *"average."* Average marks. Average looks. Average potential. It wasn't cruel — it was just the quiet, dismissive way her family treated her.

At 17, something shifted. Her art teacher told her, *"The way you see the world is different — that's not average, it's rare."*

That one comment sparked a shift. She started sketching daily, then created an Instagram page. Slowly, her following grew. By 20, she was freelancing for local brands and saving for her own studio.

She still heard the old voices sometimes. But they no longer held the final say.

Spiritual and Psychological Imperatives to Rise

From a spiritual perspective, you were not created to remain hidden.

No matter your faith or background, the message echoes across traditions: you are fearfully and wonderfully made. You are called to *steward* your life — not bury it in fear, shame, or smallness.

When you stay small, the world loses something only *you* could have brought.

From a psychological standpoint, self-actualization — becoming who you were meant to be — is one of the deepest human needs. It's not a luxury; it's a responsibility.

Think of it this way: your life is a gift. What you do with it is your response to that gift. Staying stuck in low self-esteem doesn't just hurt you — it affects your relationships, your work, your legacy.

Choosing to rise is choosing to live with honor — for yourself, and for the people whose lives your confidence will touch.

Action Plan: The "Enough Is Enough" Declaration

It's time to make your turning point *tangible*.

This is not just about reading words. This is about *writing your resolve*. I want you to grab a journal or a piece of paper. Sit somewhere quiet. And complete this declaration in your own words.

My *"Enough Is Enough"* Declaration
I have lived long enough in self-doubt, silence, and fear.
I have accepted less, played small, and avoided the mirror.
But today, I draw a line.
Enough with shrinking to make others comfortable.
Enough with believing lies spoken years ago.
Enough with putting my worth on sale for approval.
I was not born to stay in the background.
I am not broken. I am not too late. I am not disqualified.
I am worthy of love, purpose, respect, and joy — simply because I exist.
Starting today, I choose to rise.
I will speak kindly to myself.
I will pursue the dreams I've shelved.
I will show up — not perfectly, but fully.
I don't need permission. I only need a decision.
And I've made it.
I rise — for myself, for my future, for the life I was born to live.

(Signed) ____________________________
(Date) ______________________________

(Print it. Frame it. Read it aloud every morning for the next 7 days. Let it break through old programming. Let it awaken something holy and fierce within you.)

The next chapter will guide you into the benefits of living with high self-esteem — not just what it does for you, but what it allows you to *give* to the world around you. But for now — take a deep breath.
You've just taken the most important step:
You've decided to rise.

Chapter 6:
Benefits of a High Positive Self-Esteem

Imagine waking up and not feeling like you're already behind. Imagine looking into the mirror and seeing someone worth loving, worth listening to, and worth investing in. Imagine walking into a room and not needing to prove your worth — just *being* enough.

That's what high positive self-esteem feels like. It's not arrogance, ego, or denial of flaws. It's the deep, steady knowing that you are valuable — not because of what you do, but because of who you are.

In this chapter, we're going to explore what happens when self-esteem is no longer a struggle, but a source of strength. These are not motivational slogans, but lived realities — changes that affect every part of your life once you begin to see yourself through a healthy lens.

Greater Resilience and Mental Strength

Life will throw punches. No amount of positive thinking can prevent hardship. But the difference between those who bounce back and those who stay broken often lies in *how they see themselves* in the face of failure.

People with high self-esteem don't crumble when criticized, rejected, or corrected — because their worth isn't hanging on one moment. They know that one failure doesn't define their identity.

Take Jitesh, a marketing executive who was passed over for a promotion he had been working toward for over a year. Initially, he was devastated. But instead

of spiraling into self-loathing like he once would have, he took a day off, reflected on the feedback, and met with his manager to discuss a growth plan.
"I realized I didn't get the role," he told me, *"but I didn't lose myself. There's a difference. That's new for me."*
Resilience isn't just about strength. It's about *knowing your value doesn't vanish* when life doesn't go your way. High self-esteem gives you a rooted sense of identity — you may bend, but you don't break.

Healthier Relationships and Boundaries
One of the first places high self-esteem shows up is in how we love — and let ourselves be loved.
People with strong self-worth don't chase validation in relationships. They don't tolerate disrespect under the excuse of love. They don't stay silent to keep the peace while losing themselves in the process.
Instead, they:

- ✓ Know what they bring to the table.
- ✓ Speak their needs clearly, without fear.
- ✓ Walk away from relationships that drain or devalue them.
- ✓ Attract partners and friends who celebrate, not control them.

Swati, a 29-year-old schoolteacher, had spent years in a relationship where she was constantly criticized — her body, her career, even her laugh. When she began working on herself, reading, journaling, and affirming her worth, something shifted.
"I used to think if I left him, I'd be alone forever. But now I see — being alone isn't the worst thing. Losing myself is."

She left the relationship. And for the first time, she started choosing herself. High self-esteem gave her not just courage, but *clarity* — clarity that love should never require shrinking who you are.

Increased Productivity and Career Growth

A person with high self-esteem works differently.

They are not always the loudest in the room. But they show up with quiet confidence. They take ownership. They ask questions. They admit when they don't know, without shame. And they celebrate their wins — without waiting for others to clap first.

Nikhil, a junior analyst, used to hide behind his desk. He rarely spoke up, even when he had strong ideas. After working through a self-coaching program, he began to shift.

One day during a team meeting, he made a suggestion that significantly cut report-processing time. His manager was impressed. That small act gave Nikhil the confidence to share more. Six months later, he was asked to mentor new joiners — not because he was the smartest, but because he had finally started believing in his voice.

High self-esteem doesn't guarantee success. But it *positions you for it.* You stop disqualifying yourself before others even get a chance to see your worth.

You begin showing up as if you belong — because deep inside, you've finally accepted that you do.

Inner Peace and Reduced Anxiety

Low self-esteem is mentally exhausting. The constant overthinking, comparison, need for validation, fear of rejection — it takes a toll.

When you start building a healthier self-view, something beautiful happens: *the noise quiets down.*

You stop needing to over-explain.
You stop rehearsing every conversation in your head.
You stop living on edge, terrified of being judged.
You feel free — not because life is perfect, but because *you're no longer fighting yourself every day.*
Maya, a graphic designer, once shared, *"Earlier, even when nothing was wrong, I felt anxious — like I had to prove something just to exist. Now, I wake up and feel calm. Not because everything's okay outside, but because I'm okay inside."*
High self-esteem gives you peace of mind — not perfection of life.

Real-Life Example: How Positive Esteem Helped Tina Build Her Business After Failure

Tina had always wanted to start a handmade candle business. After completing a weekend entrepreneurship program, she pooled her savings, designed her first batch, and launched her brand online.
But within four months, sales dipped, customer feedback was mixed, and she started doubting the entire venture.
Her first instinct? Quit.
But then, she remembered what her mentor once told her: *"Your business failing doesn't mean you are a failure."*
That sentence became her lifeline.
Tina paused. She didn't give up — she regrouped. She reached out to a few loyal customers, asked for feedback, redesigned her product line, and rebranded.
Within a year, her business not only recovered but tripled in sales. Today, Tina conducts workshops for

women entrepreneurs and credits her *belief in herself* — not luck or funding — as the turning point.
"I failed," she says, *"but I didn't disappear. That's what changed everything."*

Worksheet: Visualize Your Esteemed Life
Let's bring this home with a short but powerful exercise.
Get a journal and answer the following, in your own words — without filters, fear, or 'shoulds.'
1. *If I truly believed I was worthy and enough, I would…*
(Example: apply for the lead role, say no to toxic friends, dress the way I want, speak my truth.)
2. *Three areas of my life where high self-esteem would change everything are…*
(Think of relationships, career, health, creativity, finances.)
3. *What does the "high self-esteem version" of me do differently every day?*
How does this version talk, walk, work, love, rest, and lead?
4. *Write one sentence of affirmation from this "higher self" to the you reading this right now:*
"Dear [Your Name], I want you to know…"

You Are Not Becoming Someone New — You Are Returning to Who You Really Are
Building positive self-esteem is not about faking confidence or forcing smiles. It's about *returning* to the truth that was always yours, before the world told you otherwise.
As you walk this path, remember — the world doesn't need a louder you. It needs a more *authentic* you. A

version of you who doesn't wait to be picked, approved, or perfect to start showing up fully.
High self-esteem doesn't make you invincible.
It makes you *available* — to your purpose, to your gifts, to your people, and to yourself.
You're not far. You're just a few courageous steps away.
In the next chapter, we will go deeper into *how* to build and sustain high self-esteem — day by day, word by word, choice by choice.
But for now, pause. Breathe.
And whisper this to yourself:
"I am allowed to take up space in this world — fully, freely, and faithfully."

Chapter 7: The Process of Rebuilding Self-Esteem A Daily Commitment

Rebuilding self-esteem isn't about a single breakthrough or a one-time pep talk. It's about slow, deliberate change — the kind that happens quietly in the background of everyday life.

Think of it like strengthening a weak muscle. You don't go to the gym once and expect to be fit. You show up consistently, even when the progress is invisible. Especially then.

That's what rebuilding your self-esteem requires: a commitment, not a crash course.

This chapter is your practical blueprint — a daily rhythm to break old beliefs, reclaim your voice, and rewire your identity. The journey begins with four key steps, followed by powerful rituals and tracking tools to keep you rooted.

Step 1: Awareness – Catching the Negative Voices

You can't change what you can't see. So the first step in this healing journey is to become aware of the invisible soundtrack playing in your mind all day long — the one that whispers, judges, and distorts reality.

Megha, a finance intern, used to call herself "stupid" every time she made a small mistake — even ones others brushed off. She'd say it under her breath, often without realizing it. In a single week, she said *"I'm so dumb"* nearly ten times. It became her default response to discomfort.

In our coaching session, I asked her to start writing down every time she said something negative about herself. The first two days were shocking to her. She filled two pages. But something powerful happened: she became conscious.

Once you hear the voice, you can challenge it. Awareness doesn't silence the critic immediately, but it puts you back in control of the volume.

Daily Practice: Carry a small notebook or use your phone's notes app. For one week, track every critical or judgmental thought you say to yourself. No need to change it — just record it. Label them "old scripts." Awareness is the first form of resistance.

Step 2: Acceptance – Releasing the Shame

Once you notice the voices, the temptation is to fight them with even more criticism.

"I shouldn't think like this."

"Why can't I be stronger?"

But self-esteem isn't built through self-punishment. It's built through acceptance.

This doesn't mean you accept the lies. It means you accept that you have wounds, conditioning, and pain that formed them — and that doesn't make you weak. It makes you human.

Rakesh, a 40-year-old manager, broke down during a seminar when we discussed emotional neglect. *"I didn't even realize I was carrying shame from my childhood,"* he said. *"My dad never told me he was proud of me. And somehow, I believed I wasn't enough. I always felt I had to prove I deserved space."*

In that moment, he didn't try to fix anything. He just sat with it. Felt it. Named it. And let it go — a little at a time.

Healing doesn't always look like victory. Sometimes, it looks like sitting beside your pain without judgment.
Reflection Prompt: Take a few quiet minutes and write a letter to yourself — not to fix, justify, or improve anything — but simply to say, *"I see you. I understand why you feel this way. And I'm here for you."*
The shame loses power when met with compassion.

Step 3: Affirmation – Rewriting the Narrative
Now comes the rewriting.
Affirmations are more than positive phrases. When used intentionally, they become counter-spells to the curses you've unconsciously repeated for years.
But for them to work, they must be:

- ✓ Believable — just enough to stretch you, not scare you.
- ✓ Consistent — like water over stone, day by day.

Take Karishma. She used to say, *"I'm not leadership material."* That belief came from years of being overlooked and a boss who once said she was *"too emotional."* Together, we built a counter-affirmation: *"My empathy is my leadership strength."*
She wrote it on a sticky note, placed it on her laptop, and repeated it every morning before work. After two months, she led her first project team.
That's not magic — it's reprogramming.
The mind believes what it hears repeatedly — even if it started as a lie. You have the power to give it truth instead.

Step 4: Action – Daily Esteem-Building Practices
Words are powerful — but actions confirm identity.

To rebuild your self-esteem, you need to collect evidence every day that you are someone worth respecting — and that means doing things your old self might avoid.

- ✓ Say no to something just to honor your boundaries.
- ✓ Speak up in a meeting, even if your voice shakes.
- ✓ Finish a task you've been avoiding — not for perfection, but for self-trust.
- ✓ Take care of your body — not to look a certain way, but to value yourself.

Rahul, a 26-year-old junior associate, started small. He began making his bed each morning, something he never used to bother with. *"It felt silly at first,"* he admitted. *"But now, it's the first win of the day. It tells me I'm worth living in a clean, peaceful space."*

Small wins build big self-respect.

Key Shift: Don't wait to feel confident to take action. Take action to become confident. That's how esteem is earned — *from you, to you.*

Morning Rituals & Evening Reflections

Here's a simple but transformative structure to support your journey:

Mornings: Begin with Intention

Start your day by stating:

- ✓ One affirmation about yourself.
- ✓ One thing you're grateful for.
- ✓ One small goal for the day.

Example:

"I am worthy of respect."

"I am grateful for my voice."

"Today, I will speak up once without apology."

This sets your internal compass before the world's voices try to pull you off course.

Evenings: Reflect with Compassion

End your day by answering:

- ✓ *What did I do well today?*
- ✓ *Where did I catch myself being critical?*
- ✓ *What can I forgive myself for?*
- ✓ *What will I carry forward tomorrow?*

This reflection softens guilt, builds awareness, and strengthens your inner parent — the one who sees, corrects, and affirms with love.

Practice Journal: "What I Did Well Today"

This may sound simple, but it is revolutionary for someone used to self-criticism.

Each night, write three things you did well that day. They don't have to be heroic.

- ✓ *"I ate a good lunch instead of skipping."*
- ✓ *"I asked for help at work without shame."*
- ✓ *"I caught myself spiraling and paused."*

Doing this consistently helps you build a new narrative — one rooted in evidence that you are growing.

Over time, your mind begins to scan for success instead of failure — and that changes everything.

Sample Weekly Affirmation Tracker

Here's a structure you can recreate in your journal, phone notes, or printable worksheet.

Day	**Affirmation**	**Did I say it aloud today?**	**Did I act on it?**	**Notes / Feelings**
Monday	I am worthy of love and rest.	☑ Yes	☑ Took a nap	Felt guilty at first, but better later
Tuesday	My voice matters in every room.	☑ Yes	✗ Stayed silent	Will try again tomorrow
Wednesday	I am growing, even when it's messy.	☑ Yes	☑ Spoke honestly	Felt lighter after that conversation
Thursday	I am not behind; I'm on my path.	☑ Yes	☑ Made a plan	Progress feels real today
Friday	My boundaries are a gift to myself.	☑ Yes	☑ Said no	Nervous, but proud
Saturday	I celebrate my progress without guilt	☑ Yes	☑ Shared win	Felt bold but good
Sunday	I am enough — nothing to prove.	☑ Yes	☑ Rested freely	Peaceful day

Chapter 8: Guarding Your Esteem – Handling Criticism and Setbacks

Building self-esteem is one part of the journey. Protecting it—in the real, raw, reactive world—is another. It's one thing to affirm your worth in the quiet of your journal; it's another to hold on to it when someone challenges your competence, ignores your input, or tears you down in front of others.

If self-esteem is a house, then criticism, rejection, and failure are like storms. They don't have to destroy the structure—but only if that house has a strong foundation, reinforced walls, and regular care.

This chapter is about equipping you with practical ways to defend your inner worth in the face of external challenges. Because no matter how healed or grounded you become, life won't stop being hard. But *you* will get stronger in how you handle it.

Constructive vs. Destructive Criticism

Let's begin by calling out something most of us were never taught: Not all criticism is equal. Some of it is meant to build. Some of it is meant to break.

- ✓ Constructive criticism is rooted in care. It may be direct or even uncomfortable, but its intention is to help you grow. It focuses on actions, not identity. It gives you a path forward.
- ✓ Destructive criticism, on the other hand, is often rooted in someone else's insecurity, control, or pain. It attacks your character, not

your behavior. It leaves you feeling smaller, not sharper.

Here's the test:

- ✓ Constructive says: "Here's what didn't work and how to improve it."
- ✓ Destructive says: "You're not good enough. You never get it right."

I once worked with a young professional named Deepak. He had presented a project to his department that he'd spent weeks preparing. After the presentation, his manager told him in front of others, *"You talk too much, and your slides were useless."*

Deepak froze. For days, he spiraled into doubt, questioning his value and ability.

When we spoke, I asked him, *"Was that feedback specific or useful?"* He paused and said, *"No. He never told me what to change, just that I failed."*

That was a turning point for Deepak. He began separating feedback from insult, truth from tone. And that helped him protect his esteem.

Guardrail Principle: *Always evaluate the <u>intention</u>, <u>tone</u>, and <u>usefulness</u> of feedback before <u>internalizing it</u>.* Not everyone's words deserve a place in your identity.

Learning to Say No Without Guilt

Saying "no" is one of the most important ways to guard your self-worth. And yet, for many of us raised to please, agree, and serve, "no" feels like betrayal.

But here's the truth: every time you say "yes" to something that drains you, just to keep the peace, you say "no" to your own self-respect.

Anjali, a bright and sincere mid-level team leader, used to accept every additional task thrown her way.

She worked weekends, stayed late, even did her teammate's work—just to be liked. But inside, she was exhausted and resentful.

One afternoon, when her boss asked her to take over someone else's presentation—again—she finally said, *"I'm afraid I can't this time. My plate is full, and I want to do justice to what I've already taken on."*

She expected backlash. Instead, her boss respected her more. And she walked away lighter.

Saying no with grace isn't rebellion. It's self-respect in action.

When you begin to value your time, energy, and boundaries, your esteem rises naturally—because you're treating yourself the way you wish others would.

Handling Rejection with Maturity

Rejection stings. Whether it's a failed interview, a friend who drifts away, or a proposal that's turned down—it touches something deep. Often, it revives old beliefs: *You're not wanted. You're not enough.*

But what if rejection wasn't personal?

What if it was just redirection?

Kiran, a young entrepreneur, once pitched his idea to five investors in a week—and got five polite "no's." His first instinct? *"Maybe I'm not cut out for this."*

But after talking to a mentor, he decided to reframe: *"If this isn't the right fit, maybe it's because I'm meant to refine something before the yes comes."*

He improved his pitch. Six weeks later, one investor said yes—and it changed his trajectory.

Here's the key: ***Rejection is information, not identity.***

It might mean your idea needs more work. Or that the timing is wrong. Or simply that this opportunity wasn't *your* door. But it never means *you* are less worthy.

High self-esteem doesn't shield you from rejection. It helps you move through it without losing yourself.

Shielding Esteem in Difficult Work Environments

Some people work in places where respect, recognition, and empathy are in short supply. In such settings, protecting your self-esteem becomes both harder—and more essential.

Joel's story is a perfect example.

Case Study: Joel's Experience with a Toxic Manager

Joel, an operations executive in his early 30s, had just joined a reputed firm. He was sharp, proactive, and well-liked by peers. But his manager, Vikram, had a different approach: controlling, dismissive, and often cruel.

During meetings, Vikram would interrupt Joel mid-sentence. He rarely acknowledged his efforts and frequently took credit for Joel's ideas. Once, after Joel worked overnight on a client deck, Vikram tossed it aside and said, *"I expected better from someone with your experience."*

At first, Joel internalized the criticism. He worked harder, stayed longer, tried to "earn" respect. But nothing changed. One evening, after a particularly harsh meeting, Joel broke down.

That night, he made a decision: *"I can't control Vikram, but I can stop letting him decide who I am."*

Here's what Joel did next:

He began journaling every compliment or success he experienced, no matter how small.

He sought feedback from others in the team to gain a balanced perspective.

He created a *"Self-Worth File"* where he stored appreciation emails, notes from clients, and personal wins.

He started therapy to work through his patterns of seeking approval from authority figures.

Eventually, he requested a transfer to another team—and thrived.

Joel's esteem didn't come from changing Vikram. It came from changing **his own voice** inside.

When your external world is harsh, your internal world must become a sanctuary. That's how esteem is preserved in unfriendly places.

Action Plan: The *"Response Over Reaction"* Formula

Here's a practical framework that you can start applying immediately when your esteem is under attack — at work, in relationships, or within yourself.

Step 1: Pause. Don't React.

When you receive criticism or feel rejected, take 5 seconds. Breathe.

That pause breaks the autopilot of reacting from old wounds.

Step 2: Ask – *"What's the truth here?"*

Evaluate the situation:

- ✓ Is this feedback specific, or is it an attack?
- ✓ Is it about your work, or is it someone's projection?
- ✓ What *might* be true? What's not?
- ✓ Separate fact from feeling.

Step 3: Respond from Power, Not Pain

Choose your response intentionally. That might look like:

- ✓ Asking for clarification.
- ✓ Standing up with grace.
- ✓ Letting it go without internalizing.
- ✓ Saying, "Thank you, I'll think about that," and moving on.

Step 4: Restore Your Inner Voice

After the situation, do something to reconnect with your worth:

- ✓ Repeat an affirmation ("This doesn't define me.")
- ✓ Journal how you handled it differently.
- ✓ Call someone who sees the best in you.
- ✓ Reflect on past victories.

Remember: The situation is temporary. Your self-worth is not.

Closing Encouragement: Not Everyone Will See You – That's Okay

You will be misunderstood. Criticized. Overlooked. That's part of life.

But your job is *not* to convince the world of your worth.

Your job is to believe it so clearly that the world's opinion no longer decides how you show up.

- ✓ You can learn from feedback without being destroyed by it.
- ✓ You can walk away from disrespect without feeling guilty.
- ✓ You can fail and still look yourself in the mirror and say, *"You're still worthy. Still valuable. Still enough."*

That's what guarding your esteem looks like in the real world. And it's one of the strongest things you'll ever do.

In the another chapter, we'll explore how to help others build their self-esteem—because once you've tasted freedom, it's impossible not to want the same for others.

But for now, one last truth to remember:

"Your worth was never meant to be debated. Only discovered, embraced, and defended with love."

Chapter 9:
Building Esteem in the Workplace

Walk into any office, factory, classroom, or boardroom, and you'll feel it — an invisible atmosphere that tells you whether people feel safe, seen, and valued... or small, tense, and afraid to fail.

That atmosphere isn't created by the furniture or logos on the wall. It's shaped by the collective self-esteem of the individuals inside it — and more importantly, by how that esteem is either nurtured or neglected by the culture.

Self-esteem isn't something we leave at the door when we enter the workplace. We bring it with us — in how we communicate, take initiative, respond to setbacks, receive feedback, and lead or follow.

Whether you're a new employee, a middle manager, or the CEO — you have both the *responsibility and the opportunity* to influence the self-worth climate of your workplace.

This chapter explores how organizations affect esteem, how individuals can strengthen their self-worth in high-pressure settings, and how leaders can build a culture where people rise — not shrink.

How Organizations Impact Self-Esteem

For many people, work is more than just a paycheck — it's a place where their identity, purpose, and capability are constantly being shaped.

A workplace can be a platform for growth and confidence, or a breeding ground for insecurity and silent resignation.

Ritika's story illustrates this well.

The Story of Ritika: Esteem at a Crossroads

Ritika joined a fast-growing retail firm as a sales associate. On paper, it was a great role: growing company, decent salary, chances for advancement.

But the reality felt different.

Her team leader rarely acknowledged effort, only pointing out mistakes. In team huddles, performance comparisons were harsh and public. Despite meeting monthly targets, Ritika often felt invisible.

One day, after being scolded for a minor delay in report submission, she confided in a colleague, *"I feel like I'm always walking on eggshells. Like I'm only as good as my last performance."*

It wasn't the job that was destroying her confidence. It was the environment — one that praised numbers but forgot the people behind them.

Six months later, Ritika left.

Contrast that with her next job at a smaller firm. There, her new manager scheduled one-on-ones every month just to ask: *How are you doing? What's one thing I can do to support you better?*

In the first team meeting, the manager thanked Ritika for bringing in new client leads, even before they converted to business.

She felt seen. Encouraged. Empowered.

In less than a year, she rose to team lead — not because she had changed, but because the culture had.

For Employees: Building Self-Worth in a Competitive Culture

If you're in a job that feels stressful, competitive, or dismissive of your individuality, don't wait for someone else to affirm you. Begin where you are.

The workplace might not always change — but your relationship with yourself can.

Take Ownership of Your Inner Voice

Start noticing how you speak to yourself after a mistake, or before a presentation. Are you fueling fear or feeding confidence?

Instead of: *"I'm not ready for this,"*

Say: *"I may not know everything, but I'm willing to grow and learn."*

Track Internal Wins

Keep a "Work Journal" or a digital note where you list one small win each day:

- ✓ A conversation you handled well.
- ✓ A task you completed on time.
- ✓ A client who responded positively.

This helps build an internal file of progress you can draw from when esteem dips.

Seek Growth, Not Just Praise

Esteem doesn't grow from applause alone. It grows when you challenge yourself, learn new skills, and see yourself improve over time.

Sign up for a workshop. Volunteer for a small leadership role. Mentor a colleague. Every stretch adds a brick to your internal foundation.

Set Boundaries Without Guilt

High self-esteem shows up when you can say:

- ✓ *"I'm available till 6 pm."*
- ✓ *"I'd like to clarify expectations before I begin."*
- ✓ *"I appreciate feedback, but I'd prefer it one-on-one."*

These aren't rude. They're respectful — to you and to others.

For Managers: Fostering Esteem in Teams

As a manager, you are not just managing **tasks** — you're managing **people**. And people perform at their best when they feel psychologically safe and emotionally valued.

Here are ways you can become a builder of esteem within your team — whether you lead two or two hundred.

Catch Them Doing Right

Too often, feedback is reactive — given only when things go wrong. Flip the script.

Start every week by sending a short appreciation message to at least one team member. Notice effort, not just results.

A single sentence like, *"I saw how you stayed late to help with that last-minute report. That's real ownership,"* can shift someone's entire self-view.

Make Feedback Growth-Oriented

Don't say: *"This is not good enough."*

Say: *"Here's what's missing, and how you can strengthen it next time."*

Affirm identity even while correcting behavior:

"I know you care about details — let's make sure that reflects in this version."

Encourage Voice, Not Just Compliance

Invite opinions from quieter team members. Acknowledge new ideas. Celebrate risks, even if the outcome wasn't perfect.

Self-esteem grows when people feel **trusted** to contribute beyond their job description.

Don't Just Lead Performance — Lead People

Know their birthdays. Ask about their family. Check in on their well-being during difficult seasons. Leadership is not just about results; it's about relationship.

Culture of Encouragement: A Leadership Responsibility

Culture isn't created in HR meetings or vision statements. It's created in hallway conversations, performance reviews, emails, and the way leaders respond to failure.

When encouragement becomes part of the fabric, self-esteem becomes a norm, not an exception.

A team that feels safe is a team that will:

- ✓ Speak the truth instead of what they think the boss wants to hear.
- ✓ Innovate without fear of ridicule.
- ✓ Stay longer, care deeper, and perform better.

High-esteemed teams don't happen by accident. They are cultivated intentionally — from the top down and the inside out.

Sample: "High Esteem Workplace Charter"

This sample charter can be adapted by any company, team, or individual leader to reinforce a culture of psychological safety and self-worth.

High Esteem Workplace Charter

We, as a team, commit to:

- ✓ ***Respect Everyone's Worth*** – *Every person here is valuable, regardless of their title, tenure, or background.*
- ✓ ***Celebrate Effort and Growth*** – *We recognize and acknowledge the progress, not just perfection.*
- ✓ ***Give Feedback with Empathy*** – *Our feedback will always focus on behaviors, never on belittling.*

- ✓ ***Encourage Expression** – We welcome diverse voices and create space for people to speak without fear.*
- ✓ ***Support Boundaries** – We respect personal time, mental space, and work-life dignity.*
- ✓ ***Model Esteem from Leadership** – Our managers and leaders will set the tone of encouragement and openness.*
- ✓ ***Correct Without Shaming** – We believe in accountability, delivered with dignity.*
- ✓ ***Grow Together** – We see every team member as a builder of culture, not just a performer of tasks.*

Signed,
(Leader Name)
(Team Name)
(Date)

Exercise: Writing Your Professional Self-Worth Statement

Take a quiet 15 minutes. Reflect on your value — beyond titles, numbers, or roles. Answer the prompt below in your journal or type it out and keep it in your desk drawer.

My Professional Self-Worth Statement

I am more than my job title. I bring not just skills, but heart, thought, and commitment to my work.
I may not know everything, but I learn quickly and give fully.
I add value not just through my outputs, but through how I make people feel in meetings, emails, and collaborations.

I am worthy of respect, fair treatment, and growth opportunities.
Even when I make mistakes, I remain a person of worth and integrity.
I do not need to overwork, over-please, or over-apologize to justify my role.
I am here because I belong.
And I am becoming more confident, capable, and free every day.

(Signed) ____________________
(Date) ______________________

Closing Reflections

The workplace doesn't just run on KPIs, strategy, or meetings. It runs on people — and those people rise or shrink based on how they feel about themselves and how they're treated.

When self-esteem becomes part of the organizational DNA, everything changes.

- ✓ Retention improves.
- ✓ Innovation flourishes.
- ✓ Toxicity shrinks.

And most of all, people stop surviving work and start thriving in it.

It doesn't start with policy. It starts with people like you, deciding to bring honor, empathy, and esteem into every role, every relationship, every room.

Chapter 10: Helping Others Build Their Self-Esteem

It's one thing to build your own self-esteem. It's another to help someone else rise. But both are deeply connected.

When you begin to live from a place of security, value, and truth, it becomes almost impossible not to see the brokenness in others — and want to reach out.

A teenager hiding behind sarcasm.

A junior employee afraid to speak.

A spouse who constantly apologizes.

A team that performs just enough to avoid being blamed.

Even a parent who dismisses every compliment as untrue.

We're surrounded by people who have been quietly damaged — not always by dramatic trauma, but by a thousand subtle messages that told them: "You're not enough."

This chapter is a call to be different — to be a builder of esteem in your home, your classroom, your office, your conversations.

Recognizing Low Esteem in Others

Low self-esteem isn't always loud or obvious. Often, it hides beneath humor, overachievement, passivity, or withdrawal.

Here are some common signs — not to diagnose, but to help you develop *empathy over judgment*:

- ✓ They apologize for things that don't require apologies.
- ✓ They reject compliments quickly ("No, I'm not good at that…").
- ✓ They defer constantly, even when they have good ideas.
- ✓ They laugh off their needs or feelings.
- ✓ They struggle to make eye contact or speak confidently.
- ✓ They settle — for roles, relationships, and respect that are far below what they deserve.

Once you learn to see beyond performance and posture, you begin to notice the quiet ache that says, *"I don't think I matter."*

You don't need to fix people. You simply need to *see them differently*, and treat them in a way that slowly invites them to do the same.

Being a Mirror of Strength

We become mirrors to those around us.

When someone is unsure of themselves, one of the most powerful things we can do is reflect back what is good, strong, and whole about them — even when they can't see it yet.

That's how esteem begins to rise.

Think of Neha, a single mother who returned to college in her 40s. She was in one of my evening communication classes, always sitting quietly in the back row, rarely volunteering to speak.

One evening after class, I pulled her aside and said, *"I've watched how carefully you listen. Your observations are sharp. Would you consider sharing in tomorrow's session?"*

She shook her head. *"I'm not as educated as the others. I don't want to sound stupid."*

I said gently, *"You have more life experience than most of them. Don't confuse your silence with lack of wisdom."*
The next evening, she spoke up. Tentatively, at first. Then with growing clarity. Her confidence grew steadily — and it wasn't because I taught her a new skill. It was because someone saw her *before she saw herself.*
To be a mirror of strength means you reflect someone's value *until they recognize it for themselves.*

Encouragement and Language That Uplifts
Words create worlds. Especially for those whose internal dialogue has been harsh for years.
The language we use with others — particularly in moments of failure, fear, or hesitation — can become turning points in their self-story.
Avoid:

- ✓ *"You always mess this up."*
- ✓ *"Why can't you be more like…?"*
- ✓ *"I knew you'd struggle with this."*
- ✓ *"It's not a big deal, just do it."*

These phrases, though common, can reinforce shame or incompetence.
Instead, try:

- ✓ *"This is hard, but I see you trying — and that matters."*
- ✓ *"You don't need to get it perfect. Just keep going."*
- ✓ *"That mistake doesn't define you."*
- ✓ *"I believe in your ability to grow."*

It may seem small. But I've seen lives change because someone heard, for the first time: *"You're capable. You belong. You're enough."*

Teaching Children to Develop Esteem from the Start

The best time to build self-esteem is childhood. But if you weren't raised with it, don't worry — the second-best time is *now*, through the children in your care.

Here are a few guiding principles that work whether you're a parent, teacher, mentor, or caregiver.

1. Praise Effort, Not Just Outcome

Instead of: *"You're so smart!"*

Say: *"I saw how hard you worked to solve that."*

This builds esteem based on resilience, not perfection.

2. Encourage Expression, Not Suppression

Make it safe for children to express their feelings without ridicule or punishment. Let them feel angry, sad, afraid — and teach them how to process, not suppress.

3. Let Them Try and Fail

Protecting children from all discomfort delays their development. Let them experience challenge — and then remind them: "You are strong enough to try again."

4. Be the Voice They'll Hear Later

Your words now will become their inner voice later.

A 12-year-old who hears, *"I trust you to figure it out,"* grows into an adult who tells themselves, *"I can handle this."*

Practical Tools for Mentors and Coaches

Whether you're a workplace mentor, sports coach, youth leader, or spiritual guide — your influence can be a lifeline to someone's emerging self-esteem.

Here's how to use your role effectively:

- ✓ Create Safe Spaces

Let people know that with you, they don't need to perform. They can be real. When someone knows they won't be judged or belittled, they begin to open up — and grow.

- ✓ Model Healthy Esteem
  Your self-talk becomes their blueprint. Speak with humility, not self-deprecation. Own your flaws without shame. Show them that strength and softness can coexist.
- ✓ Set Goals Together
  Let your mentees set their own goals, then help them track and celebrate progress. Let success be defined not by results, but by courage to act.
- ✓ Don't Do It *For* Them
  It's tempting to rescue. But real esteem is built by letting someone figure it out — even if it means watching them struggle a bit. You're not here to make it easy. You're here to make it *possible*.

Case Study: A Manager Who Turned Around a Team Through Esteem

Rajeev took over a floundering customer support team in a mid-sized logistics company. Performance was low, morale lower.

In his first month, he noticed something: the previous manager had ruled by fear. Every mistake was broadcast. Every win ignored.

Rajeev decided to do things differently.

First, he scheduled private 1-on-1s with each team member. Not to discuss performance, but to ask:

- ✓ *What's one thing you're proud of?*
- ✓ *What motivates you?*
- ✓ *What's one change you'd like to see?*

For many, it was the first time they were even asked.
Next, he introduced a "Win Wall" — a public board where team members could write each other appreciation notes or share positive customer feedback.
He also implemented "Failure Fridays," where the team shared one mistake they made that week — and what they learned. No shame. Just growth.
Six months later, absenteeism dropped. Ticket closures improved. And for the first time in over a year, the team exceeded its quarterly target.
But Rajeev didn't just improve performance.
He gave people back their belief in themselves.
As one of his team members said during a feedback session:
"We stopped working out of fear. We started working because we felt like we mattered."
That's the power of esteem-based leadership.

Final Words: The Gift of Helping Someone Rise
You don't need to be a psychologist or a motivational speaker to help someone build self-esteem.
You just need to care.
To listen longer. Speak gentler. Believe sooner. Encourage often.
And most of all — to treat people not as they are, but as they *could become*, if someone simply believed in them long enough for them to believe in themselves.
Helping others grow doesn't diminish your own light. It amplifies it.
Because when one person begins to rise in self-worth, they bring light to every room they enter.
Be that light.

Chapter 11: The Role of Faith and Spiritual Identity

In a world obsessed with performance, appearance, titles, and the applause of others, it's easy — too easy — to base our worth on fragile things. Promotions. Likes. Grades. Achievements. Praise.

But what happens when those things are stripped away? When the performance fails, the applause stops, or people walk away?

If your identity has no deeper anchor, everything collapses with it.

This is where faith enters the story — not as a side note, but as the foundation.

Because the deepest, most unshakable self-esteem isn't built from the outside in. It's built from the inside out — rooted in something greater than human approval: the truth of how God sees you.

Esteem and Our Creator: Anchoring in Unchanging Worth

You were not created by accident. You were not assembled randomly, nor defined by the labels the world has put on you.

Your worth begins not with what you've done, but whose you are.

In Genesis 1:27, we're told that God created man and woman *in His own image*. That means you carry divine DNA. A reflection of His glory. A bearer of something eternal.

Before you ever achieved anything, failed at anything, or proved anything, God declared you "very good."

The world tells us: *Prove yourself. Become something. Earn love.*

God says: *You are already mine. Already loved. Already chosen.*

True esteem flows from this: you are not what you do, you are who He says you are.

Biblical and Spiritual Affirmations of Value

Throughout Scripture, God speaks truth over our identity — truth that confronts every lie the world, others, or we ourselves have believed.

"You are fearfully and wonderfully made." – Psalm 139:14

Not half-made. Not second-class. *Wonderfully made.* Crafted by the hands of a Master Artist.

"You are God's masterpiece." – Ephesians 2:10

Not a mistake. Not mediocre. *A masterpiece.*

"You are chosen, royal, holy, and God's possession." – 1 Peter 2:9

You don't need to fight for acceptance. *You already belong.*

"There is no condemnation for those in Christ Jesus." – Romans 8:1

Your past doesn't define you. Your guilt doesn't hold you hostage. *You are free.*

When we begin to meditate on these words — not as verses to memorize, but as *identity to internalize* — something shifts.

You stop seeing yourself through the eyes of rejection and start seeing yourself through the lens of redemption.

Identity Beyond Achievements

Suresh was a high achiever. From school ranks to corporate ladders, he had always "won." But when his startup failed after three years, his self-esteem collapsed.

"I didn't just lose a business," he told me. *"I lost who I was."*

We unpacked his story — and it was clear. For years, his identity had been tied to success. As long as things went well, he felt good. When things fell apart, so did his worth.

It was only when he returned to his faith — a journey he had neglected in the busyness of ambition — that he began to rediscover his true value.

One evening, reading through the parable of the prodigal son in Luke 15, something clicked.

"I saw myself," he said. *"That even when I had lost everything, even when I had nothing to show — the Father ran to me."*

That story changed his story.

Your identity is not your job title. Or your net worth. Or your social status.

Your true identity is found in being a beloved child of God — unearned, undeserved, and unwavering.

That kind of esteem cannot be shaken, because it doesn't depend on what you do. It depends on who God is.

Prayer, Meditation, and Esteem

Prayer is not just asking for things. It's aligning your mind and heart with divine truth.

When you spend time in God's presence, you begin to see yourself through His eyes. And in His eyes, you are:

- ✓ *Chosen*

- ✓ *Called*
- ✓ *Forgiven*
- ✓ *Equipped*
- ✓ *Loved*

Sonia, a middle-aged homemaker who had silently battled years of shame and comparison, began a practice of daily prayer journaling. She would write:

One lie she had believed about herself.

A Scripture that countered that lie.

A prayer declaring truth over her day.

Over time, her language changed. Her countenance softened. Her confidence grew. Not because her circumstances had changed — but because her agreement with lies had been broken.

Meditation on God's Word does that. It renews your mind (Romans 12:2). It silences the inner critic. It replaces fear with faith.

If you've never done this before, start simply. Five minutes in the morning. Whisper a short verse aloud. Let it sink in. Say it until it feels true.

Esteem doesn't just rise by effort. It rises by revelation.

Real Testimony: How Faith Rebuilt Sonia's Broken Image

Sonia had grown up in a conservative home where silence was mistaken for submission and worth was tied to appearance and obedience.

As a child, she was often compared to her more confident sister. Teachers labeled her as "shy" and "slow." By adulthood, Sonia had internalized one belief: *I'm not enough.*

Her marriage wasn't abusive, but it wasn't affirming either. Her voice remained small. Her dreams stayed shelved.

One evening, during a women's church gathering, the speaker quoted Isaiah 43:1 — *"Fear not, for I have redeemed you. I have called you by name; you are mine."*

Sonia wept.

That night, she went home, looked in the mirror, and whispered: *"I am His. I am not forgotten."*

She began reading Scripture daily, replacing decades of mental judgment with divine truth. She joined a women's prayer circle, and eventually began mentoring younger women with similar stories.

Five years later, Sonia stood on a church stage sharing her testimony — the same voice that once trembled now firm and radiant.

"I used to shrink," she said. *"Now I stand. Because He stood for me first."*

That's what faith-rooted esteem looks like. Quiet strength. Deep dignity. The kind that cannot be taken by the world because it was never given by the world.

Action Plan: Writing a "God-Sized" View of Myself

Take time to reflect. Sit with your journal, Bible, and a heart open to truth.

Write out a personal affirmation — a "God-sized" identity statement — grounded in Scripture. Not who the world says you are. Not who your past says you are. But who God says you are.

Here's a guided prompt to help:

My True Identity in God

I am not my job title.
I am not my mistakes.
I am not my childhood wounds.
I am not what others say or think of me.

I am a child of God.
I am wonderfully made (Psalm 139:14).
I am forgiven and free (Romans 8:1).
I am chosen and called (1 Peter 2:9).
I am deeply loved (Romans 8:38-39).
I have purpose and hope (Jeremiah 29:11).
I am being transformed day by day (2 Corinthians 4:16).
Even when I feel weak, I am strong in Him.
Even when I fail, I am never forsaken.
Even when others don't see me, He does.
I am becoming more like Christ.
And that makes me priceless.

(Signed)______________________
(Date) ______________________

Closing Thoughts: Esteem That Endures

When you build your self-worth on the eternal truth of God's Word, no job loss, no breakup, no criticism, no failure, no silence — nothing — can take away your identity.

Because it's not *based* on you.
It's *rooted* in Him.
And He never changes.

You may have started this journey of self-esteem looking for approval, strength, or clarity. But now, you've found something deeper: your anchor.

May your esteem be no longer built on sand, but on the Rock.

Chapter 12: Esteem Maintenance – Keeping the Momentum

Building self-esteem is not a one-time achievement. It's not a weekend retreat, a motivational video, or even reading a powerful book.

It's a lifestyle.

Like any meaningful transformation—be it health, fitness, or faith—esteem requires regular care, nourishment, and protection.

Left unattended, even the strongest self-worth can begin to erode—quietly, slowly—through comparison, criticism, burnout, or simply forgetting the truth you once believed.

This chapter is about what happens after the breakthrough. It's about how to keep walking strong, even when life gets messy again. Because it will.

But this time, *you'll be ready.*

Avoiding the Trap of Comparison

Nothing drains esteem faster than comparison.

You were feeling good—until you opened Instagram and saw your friend on a vacation you can't afford.

Or you were proud of your promotion—until you heard your colleague got two steps higher in less time.

You were celebrating your weight loss—until someone else posted a perfect gym selfie.

Comparison is a thief. It doesn't just steal your joy. It steals your *focus.*

When you start measuring your progress against someone else's life, you shift from *gratitude to lack.*

Rohit, a successful regional sales head, once told me, *"I used to feel proud of what I'd built until I attended my MBA reunion. Suddenly, I felt small again."*

What changed?

Not his position. Not his pay. Just his perspective.

The antidote to comparison isn't complacency—it's consciousness. You must choose to *measure yourself by your own path.*

The question is not, *"Am I ahead of them?"*

It's, *"Am I ahead of who I was last month? Last year? Last season?"*

Self-esteem flourishes when you replace comparison with compassion—for yourself.

Continuous Learning and Growth

When you're learning, you're living.

Growth fuels self-esteem—not because you're trying to "be better," but because you're honoring your capacity to expand.

Think of esteem as a plant. Stagnation leads to dryness. But even small doses of nourishment—reading a book, learning a skill, having a meaningful conversation—keep it thriving.

Ayesha, a 42-year-old homemaker, had always felt *"less than"* because she hadn't pursued a formal career. After her children moved out, she decided to enroll in a community creative writing course.

"I was terrified," she admitted. "But the first time I saw my story printed in the college newsletter, something came alive inside me. I remembered—I still have something to offer."

Whether it's picking up a new hobby, deepening your spiritual practice, taking on a stretch assignment at

work, or simply reading a few pages of a good book each day—growth fuels dignity.
Because every time you invest in yourself, you say: *"I matter."*

Choosing Esteem-Filled Environments
No matter how strong you are, your environment plays a role in shaping how you feel.
Spend long enough around cynics, critics, or people who tear others down—and your light begins to dim.
But step into a room where people uplift, encourage, challenge kindly, and celebrate growth—and you start to rise.
Kunal, a junior architect, shared how his career changed after moving departments.
"The old team focused only on errors. I was constantly anxious. But my new team leader highlights what we've done well. She gives us space to learn from mistakes. I feel respected. I even speak up in meetings now."
We don't always have control over where we are. But we do have control over who we keep closest.
Protect your inner circle. Choose friendships, mentors, colleagues, and communities that build—not break.
Even digitally, curate your input. Follow accounts that inspire, not inflate. Engage in groups that empower, not compare.
Environment doesn't just affect performance. It affects identity.

Celebrating Small Wins
Big wins are rare. Small wins are daily.
One of the most powerful ways to sustain self-esteem is to notice and celebrate the little victories:

- ✓ You spoke up in a meeting when your inner voice wanted to hide.
- ✓ You resisted the urge to people-please and said “no” with grace.
- ✓ You finished a task that once overwhelmed you.
- ✓ You rested without guilt.

Each small step matters. Each deserves acknowledgment.

Meera, a young software engineer battling imposter syndrome, began a ritual: writing down one “win” at the end of each workday. At first, it felt silly. But over months, she started noticing her own growth—and trusting it.

When you acknowledge the small things, you build momentum. You teach your brain to see progress, not just problems.

And esteem grows not from giant leaps, but from consistent reminders that you are moving forward.

The Accountability Circle: Having Esteem Partners

One of the most underrated tools in esteem maintenance is *community-based accountability*.

You don’t need dozens of cheerleaders. But you do need a few safe, wise, honest people who:

- ✓ See your potential.
- ✓ Remind you of your worth when you forget.
- ✓ Challenge you with love when you shrink.
- ✓ Celebrate you without envy.

Call them esteem partners. Inner circle. Soul friends.

For Sandeep and Aaron, two corporate professionals who met in a leadership retreat, this took the form of a monthly breakfast meet-up. They discussed not just goals, but emotional and esteem health.

"What lie did I believe about myself this month?"
"What progress did I make that I almost overlooked?"
"Where did I shrink when I should've stood tall?"
"What's one thing I'll try, say, or let go of next month?"
Their check-ins became anchors. And over time, their sense of identity strengthened—not just because of what they did, but *who they did it with.*
You were never meant to walk this alone. Find your circle. Be someone else's.
Esteem grows in *relational soil.*

Monthly Esteem Audit Template
To keep your self-esteem healthy and growing, use this Monthly Esteem Audit — a simple, 30-minute reflection you can do at the end of each month.
Step 1: What Did I Do Well This Month?
List at least 3 things you're proud of. These can be actions, decisions, conversations, or emotional wins.
Step 2: Where Did I Feel Small or Triggered?
Note moments when your esteem felt shaken. Reflect on what caused it. Was it someone's words? A failure? A memory?
Step 3: What Helped Me Bounce Back?
Identify what helped restore your sense of worth. A friend? A prayer? A journal entry? A podcast? A quiet walk?
Step 4: What Lie Did I Refuse to Believe?
Capture one negative belief you overcame. Example: "I'm not capable." Replace it with a truth: "I'm learning and growing."
Step 5: What Will I Do Differently Next Month?
Choose one esteem-building action to prioritize. Maybe it's setting a boundary, applying for something new, or affirming yourself daily.

Keep your audit saved—on paper or digitally. Revisit past audits when you feel low. You'll see evidence of growth.
Because esteem doesn't just happen. It's *intentionally maintained.*

Final Words: Living Esteem, Not Just Building It
As we come to the end of this journey, here's the truth:
Your esteem isn't something you graduate from.
It's something you live with. Walk with. Practice. Protect.
Day after day.
Some days will feel confident.
Others will feel confusing.
You may stumble. Forget. Fall into old doubts.
But now, *you know the way back.*
And that's what matters.
The most powerful esteem is not the loudest—it's the most consistent.
It's the quiet courage to speak gently to yourself.
The steady strength to say, "I matter," even when others don't see it.
The deep confidence that *your value is not negotiable.*
So live that way.
Not perfectly. But fully.
From the inside out.

Chapter 13: The Esteemed Life – Signs of a Person with Positive High Self-Esteem

There is a quiet kind of strength that walks into the room—not loud, not boastful—but unmistakably solid. You sense it in the way someone carries themselves, not because they think they're better than others, but because they're no longer trying to *prove* they are.

This is the life of a person who has cultivated positive, high self-esteem. Not the shallow kind that shouts "look at me," but the rooted, radiant kind that says, *"I know who I am—and I know you matter, too."*

The journey to high self-esteem may begin in brokenness, but it matures into confidence, clarity, and contribution. In this final chapter, we explore what that life looks like in real time—how such people think, speak, behave, respond to adversity, and impact others.

Because the end goal of this journey isn't just feeling good about yourself.

It's becoming a person who lives fully, loves freely, and leads with purpose.

How They Think, Speak, and Behave

People with high self-esteem don't necessarily live in constant euphoria. But they walk through life with internal permission to be who they are—unapologetically and authentically.

Their thoughts are anchored in truth, not fear. They don't waste energy constantly questioning their worth. Instead, they invest that energy into growth, service, and joy.

They speak with integrity. Their words don't seek approval or attention, but add value. They affirm others without fearing their own light will dim. And perhaps most importantly—they speak to themselves with the same kindness they offer others.

Consider Sarah, a mid-level HR professional who once struggled deeply with self-doubt. After a season of coaching, reflection, and practical action, she no longer overexplained every decision or second-guessed every comment. In meetings, she began to share ideas with clarity. She didn't need to be the loudest voice—but when she spoke, people listened. Her confidence was quiet but contagious.

People with positive esteem aren't perfect—but they are at peace. They don't shrink to be liked or inflate to be accepted. They simply *show up as themselves*—with no mask, no shame, no need to perform.

How They Handle Crisis and Criticism

The real test of self-esteem is not how we act when things are easy. It's how we respond when they aren't.

When people with high esteem face crisis, they feel the full weight of it—just like anyone else. But they don't spiral into identity collapse. They might say:

- ✓ *"This is hard, but it doesn't define who I am."*
- ✓ *"This hurts, but I've survived worse."*
- ✓ *"I may not know how this ends, but I trust I'll rise."*

Take Kavita, who was laid off during a sudden corporate restructuring. It wasn't her fault. But the blow was still real. For a week, she allowed herself to feel the loss. But then she reminded herself: *"I am still capable. I am still valuable. I have faced rejection before and grown stronger. This doesn't erase my worth."*

Within three months, she had not only found another role but also started mentoring two other women navigating career setbacks. Her esteem allowed her to *rise and reach.*

When it comes to criticism, people with high esteem are not immune to pain—but they *filter feedback through a balanced lens.*

If it's true, they grow from it. If it's not, they release it.

They don't crumble because someone didn't approve. They listen, learn, and then return to the inner compass that keeps them centered.

Their internal narrative might go something like:

"I made a mistake. That doesn't make me a mistake."

Or, *"That feedback stung. But I know my intentions and I'm willing to improve."*

This doesn't happen overnight. It's a skill. A mindset. A muscle that's built over time—but one that separates those who merely survive from those who mature in resilience.

Influence on Others

Here's the beautiful paradox of self-esteem: the more secure you are in yourself, the less you need to make everything about yourself.

People with high self-esteem aren't preoccupied with being the center of attention. And yet, they *often become leaders,* influencers, mentors—because they create emotional space for others to grow.

They lift others without being threatened by their success. They speak encouragement where others sow envy. They create safe environments where people feel seen, heard, and empowered.

You'll find them in all walks of life:

- ✓ The teacher who doesn't just teach but *believes* in her students' greatness.
- ✓ The manager who isn't intimidated by junior talent and instead nurtures it.
- ✓ The father who affirms his children with warmth, not pressure.
- ✓ The entrepreneur who builds not just profits, but people.

When you live with positive self-esteem, your life becomes a mirror—not just reflecting your worth, but helping others discover theirs.

Living with Vision and Value

A person with high esteem doesn't drift through life reacting to whatever comes. They live intentionally—with vision and value.

They make decisions from identity, not insecurity. They pursue purpose, not popularity.

They say no without guilt. They say yes with conviction. They hold dreams not because they're trying to prove something, but because they know they have something to give.

Sanjay, once a struggling consultant weighed down by impostor syndrome, eventually started a nonprofit coaching initiative for rural students. When asked what changed, he said, *"I stopped asking, 'What will people think?' and started asking, 'What am I here for?'"*

That's the fruit of high esteem.

It's not just about success. It's about significance.

You stop chasing validation. You start creating impact.

Final Story: From Self-Doubt to Self-Worth – The Story of Deepak

Deepak grew up in the shadow of his older brother—a national-level athlete and top-tier student. At every family function, people would say, *"Why can't you be more like your brother?"*

He tried. He studied harder. Took up the same sport. But he never quite measured up.

By the time he entered his 30s, Deepak was a middle manager at a manufacturing firm. Smart, competent—but withdrawn. Afraid to speak up. Constantly overthinking.

At a leadership development workshop, he was asked to write a personal affirmation. He sat staring at his blank notepad, stuck.

That's when the facilitator walked up and said:

"Don't write what others want you to say. Write what you've always wanted to believe."

So Deepak wrote one line: *"I am enough."*

It felt strange at first. But something inside him stirred.

Over the next few months, he began working with a coach. He started tracking small wins—conversations he handled well, decisions he took ownership of. He journaled. He read. He forgave people from his past. He began attending Toastmasters to work on public speaking—not to impress, but to grow.

A year later, he was leading strategy meetings with confidence. His body language had shifted. His tone was calmer. He wasn't trying to *be* anyone else.

He had found his own voice—and it was enough.

Today, Deepak runs a small mentoring circle for young professionals with low confidence. He often tells them, *"You don't have to shout to be strong. You just need to stop whispering to yourself that you're not worthy."*

His story isn't glamorous. But it's powerful.

Because it reminds us: the road from self-doubt to self-worth is real. It's possible. And it begins with one brave choice—to believe you matter.

Conclusion: This Is Not the End

If you've reached this far, you've already done what many never do.

You've paused long enough to look inward.

You've named the lies, studied the patterns, and traced your pain.

You've chosen growth.

And maybe, for the first time, you've begun to see your reflection not with shame, but with dignity.

That's what self-esteem is. Not arrogance. Not perfection.

But the steady knowing that you are enough, worthy, capable, valuable, and ready to live *fully awake.*

Now, go live that truth.

Not one day.

Today.

Closing Section: Final Thoughts & Reader's Declaration of Esteem

You made it!

Not just to the end of a book, but to the beginning of something far more meaningful—a life where you no longer shrink, settle, or apologize for your existence.

You've read about broken beginnings and bold breakthroughs. You've confronted childhood conditioning, internal voices, cultural lies, and painful labels. You've witnessed how esteem rises slowly—brick by brick—not in perfection, but in process.

And if you're still here, something within you has shifted.

Maybe you've forgiven yourself.

Maybe you've found your voice.

Maybe you've realized that you were never really broken—just buried under years of false messages and fear.

Whatever your journey has looked like, know this:

You are not the person you were when you started.

Because you've chosen to see yourself through the lens of truth, compassion, faith, and identity.

That, dear reader, is nothing short of transformation.

And from this place of truth, we now invite you to make a personal declaration—not to impress, not to perform, but to affirm that your self-worth is no longer negotiable.

Reader's Declaration of Esteem

You may choose to read this aloud, write it down, or revisit it each week until it becomes part of you.

Today, I choose to live from truth—not from fear.

I am not defined by my past, my mistakes, or anyone's opinion of me.

I am not who they said I was. I am not what happened to me.

I am who I choose to be.

I am worthy. I am enough. I am seen.

I am capable of growth, healing, and contribution.

I will no longer apologize for taking up space.

I will stop shrinking to make others comfortable.

I will stand in my identity, speak with clarity, and walk in purpose.

I choose to see my flaws with grace and my strengths with gratitude.

I will not compare my journey to someone else's highlight reel.

I will celebrate small wins and rise from every setback.

I will speak to myself kindly.

I will forgive myself freely.

I will treat myself as someone who matters—because I do.

And when I forget, I will return to truth. Again and again.

This is my new story. And I choose to live it fully.

(Signed)______________________________

(Date) ______________________________

Appendices

Appendix A: Daily Esteem Journal Template

This journal is not about keeping a record of tasks. It's about keeping a relationship—with yourself.

Use this template each morning or evening. It can be completed in under 10 minutes, but over time, the effects compound into powerful inner transformation.

DAILY ESTEEM JOURNAL

(You can print this page or write in a notebook using the prompts below)

1. Three Words to Describe How I Feel Right Now:

---

2. One Thing I Did Today That I'm Proud Of:

---

3. One Thought That Challenged My Esteem Today:

What is the truth I choose instead?

---

4. One Win, No Matter How Small:

---

5. One Kind Thing I Will Say to Myself Before I Sleep:

---

6. One Action I Will Take Tomorrow to Honour My Worth:

(Repeat daily. Watch your esteem grow.)

Appendix B: Affirmation Cards for Students, Professionals, and Leaders

These affirmation cards can be written on index cards, displayed on mirrors, used as phone wallpapers, or read aloud each morning.

They are categorized so they speak directly into your current context—whether you are a student still discovering yourself, a working professional building confidence, or a leader shaping others.

Affirmations for Students

I am not my marks. I am more than a grade.
I have a unique voice, and it deserves to be heard.
I am growing at my own pace, and that is okay.
I am valuable—even when I don't feel noticed.
I can ask for help without feeling weak.
I am allowed to rest without guilt.
I am a work in progress—and progress is enough.

Affirmations for Professionals

- ✓ I am not my job title. I am not my paycheck.
- ✓ My worth doesn't depend on a performance review.
- ✓ I bring value to every room I enter.
- ✓ I don't have to prove myself—I just need to be myself.
- ✓ I will speak up, even if my voice shakes.
- ✓ I learn from mistakes without losing self-respect.
- ✓ I balance excellence with self-care.

Affirmations for Leaders

- ✓ I lead with integrity, not insecurity.
- ✓ My strength creates space for others to rise.

- ✓ I am not afraid of other people's greatness.
- ✓ I model self-respect so others can do the same.
- ✓ I don't need to have all the answers—I just need to listen well.
- ✓ My identity is not tied to my followers, results, or approval.
- ✓ I lead from within, not from pressure.

Final Encouragement

Dear reader, if there's one thing you carry from this book, let it be this:

Your worth was never up for debate.

You were created with value, born with purpose, and capable of greatness—not because of perfection, but because of perseverance.

Live your life not trying to become someone else, but becoming ***more of who you already are.***

And in doing so, you don't just build esteem.

You build a legacy.

About the Author
'GERARD ASSEY'

Gerard Assey is a Graduate in Economics, a PGD in Management (HRD) and holds a Doctorate in Leadership. Gerard holds several International Qualifications in Sales, Debt Collection, Training & Teaching, and is a 'Fellow' of the prestigious 'Institute of Sales & Marketing Management'-UK, a Certified NLP Practitioner, a 'Certified Trainer', an 'Accredited Management Teacher-Behavioral Sciences', a 'Certified Competency Facilitator', a 'Certified Management Consultant'- (the International credentials of a professional management consultant, awarded in accordance with global standards of the ICMCI); and a Certification from the University of Michigan in 'Successful Negotiation: Essential Strategies and Skills'

He is also a Member of the 'National Association of Sales Professionals' backed with several years experience in varied industries, both in India and Overseas. He also holds an 'Etiquette Consultant' Certification from the USA (by Sue Fox, Author of Best Seller: 'Business Etiquette for Dummies'. She has trained some of the top celebrities' world over). He was also a recipient of a scholarship for extensive training in Japan on 'Corporate Management for India'.

Gerard Assey is 'Founder & Chief Corporate Trainer' of the Group: '**Citius, Altius, Fortius Unlimited**'- an organization that **celebrated 20 years of Glorious Service** in 2021, focusing on 3 Core Competencies:

People. Performance. Profit; in functional areas of Sales & Marketing, HR & Organizational Development, covering Recruitment, Training & Consultancy!

Having managed organizations with large Sales Forces in India & Overseas, his specialization cover extensive areas of Sales Training (All levels - Presentation, Negotiation, Key/ Strategic Accounts Management & Managerial Skills for all sectors), Bid Proposal/ Capture Planning/ Management Trainings, Retail Sales, Customer Service & Customer Retention Programs, Training for Prevention & Collection of Debt, Self & Personal Development Programs (Time Management, Teamwork & Team Building, Business Etiquette & Personal Grooming, Leadership & Managerial Skills, People Management Skills, Train-the-Trainer etc), including preparation of Custom-designed Business Manuals for Internal (HR, Induction, and Sales etc) & External use (Instruction, User Manuals).

Gerard has successfully conducted over 6460 Trainings & Workshops (as of June '25) all across India, Middle East, Africa, Europe & S.E. Asia. Besides public programs conducted regularly, both in India & Overseas, he has some of the top names as clients whom he services from Single Owners to large Public & Government undertakings, covering all sectors, for their in-house needs.

His website: www.CollectionSkills.com is the only one in this part of the world to be featured in the 'Collections & Credit Risk Magazine-USA' under 'Who's Who in Training' and ranks TOP, along with other websites listed below on most search engines.

Gerard is author of 195 books already (June 2025), all the books being available on all online platforms and outlets as E-books and Paperbacks

A few of our business related books:

1. Bite-sized Bits on Commonsense Management
2. Heart to Heart on Life's Principles'
3. How to become a Successful Manager
4. The Sales Professionals' Master Workbook of S.Y.S.T.E.M.S
5. The Professional Business Email Etiquette Handbook & Guide
6. The Professional Business Video-Conferencing Etiquette Handbook & Guide
7. Professional Presentation Skills
8. Exceptional Customer Service
9. Professional Tele-Marketing Skills
10. Professional Debt Collection Skills
11. The G.R.E.A.T. Sales & Service Workbook
12. Sales Training Advantage for Results (*The Ultimate Sales Training Manual to enable you stand out as a S.T.A.R.*)
13. CEO Daily Planner & Organizer
14. The Sales Professionals' Master Daily Planner
15. The Professional Debt Collector's Master Daily Planner
16. My Daily Planner & Organizer
17. MY EMERGENCY INFORMATION RECORD (Family Emergency & Peace of Mind Planner)
18. The Ultimate Therapist & Counselors Planner and Organizer
19. Building an Ethical Workplace
20. Managing Relationships at Work
21. Managing Business Meetings Effectively
22. Effective Delegation Skills
23. Goal Setting for Success
24. B2B Selling by Email
25. Professional Business Etiquette & Grooming
26. Dining Etiquette & Table Manners
27. Effective Networking Skills
28. Grooming, Etiquette & Manners for Teens, Young Adults & Future Leaders
29. Inter-Personal Skills
30. Get Ready, Get Hired!
31. Selling in a Recession
32. Effective Receivables Management in an Economic Downturn!
33. Real Estate & Property Sales Training
34. Credit Sales & Accounts Receivable Management

35. Selling Skills for Real Estate & Property Advisors
36. Take G.R.E.A.T. C.A.R.E!
37. Spa, Salon & Health Club Selling Skills
38. Selling Travel, Holiday & MICE Services
39. Selling Skills for Spa's, Salons & Health Clubs
40. Retailing in Salons & Spas
41. Selling Holiday, Vacation, Tours & Packages
42. The Power of Sales Referrals
43. Selling Luxury
44. Technical Selling Skills
45. Financial Advisors Sales Training
46. Dealing with Burnout at Work Monopolize Your Markets
47. Selling to Affluent Customers
48. Growing up with Grace
49. Financial Selling Skills
50. *The Effective Manager's Guide: Key Skills to Thrive*
51. From Aspiring to Inspiring: A Guide for New Managers on the Rise
52. The Power of Focus
53. Selling with Integrity: Sell Like Jesus The Perfect Role Model!
54. 31 Habits of Champions: Your 31-Day Journey to Greatness
55. Rejecting Grasshopper Talk: From Grasshopper to Giant-Killer-*Defeating Giants Daily!*
56. Navigate the AI-Powered Future of Bid & Proposals: Up-Skill to Stay Relevant with Alternative Career Paths & Opportunities
57. Hiring Sales Winners
58. Present with Impact
59. Success Unlocked: *Breaking Free from Habits that Hold You Back*
60. Complaints to Cheers, Feedback to Gold: Mastering Complaints Management
61. Thriving Together: *Cultivating Diversity, Equity, and Inclusion*
62. Coaching Skills for Sales Managers
63. Soaring to Success in Business & Leadership: Swifter, Higher, Stronger!
64. From Classroom to Podium: A Student's Guide to Powerful Public Speaking & Presentation Skills
65. Developing Self-Discipline
66. The CEO's 31-Day Power Plan: Unlocking Success through Essential Traits

67. Credibility Matters
68. A Winning Attitude
69. Bid & Proposal Management Using AI
70. Sales Forecasting: A Practical & Proven Guide to Strategic Sales Forecasting
71. Elevate & Energize: *50 Dynamic & Fun Activities for Peak Workplace Morale*
72. 'Sales SOS! Sales on Fire! *30 Days to Conquer Chaos & the Nightmares of Success!'*
73. Mastering Sales Managerial Skills: *Building High-Performing Teams & Driving Exceptional Results*
74. Eagle-Eyed Leadership: Unleashing the Power of 31 Lessons from Eagles
75. The Ultimate Employee Training Guide: *Training Today, Leading Tomorrow*
76. Being More Accountable at Work
77. Creating a Culture of Continuous Improvement
78. Effective Questioning & Listening Skills
79. The Power of Value Selling
80. The Growth Mindset
81. Mastering Professional Help Desk Skills
82. The Power to Lead with Empathy
83. Being Prepared: The Key to Unlocking Success
84. Youthful Spark-Youth Energizers, Activities and Games-Igniting the Fun in Youth
85. Ignite your Motivation for Success
86. Elevate Your Executive Presence: *Your Roadmap to Executive Excellence*
87. Smart Decisions: *Mastering Problem Solving with Strategic Solutions for Business Success*
88. Strategic Planning: *Developing and Implementing Strategic Plans to Achieve Long-Term Business Goals*
89. The Power of Stay Interviews
90. Developing G.R.I.T.
91. Adaptability
92. Diagnosis- *A Key Skill for Leadership*
93. The Burnout-Proof Salesperson: *The Master Guide to Preventing Stress & Burnout-* Strategies for Thriving in Sales
94. Learning from Failure: *Keys to Success*
95. Customer Success Management
96. Overcoming the Killers of Motivation
97. The C-Suite Code: *Mastering Skills for Executive Excellence'*

98. Dealing with Difficult Customers
99. Unlocking Your Potential: Mastering the Top 20 Life Skills for a Brighter Future
100. Nurturing Tomorrow's Leaders: *Essential Soft Skills Every Child Must Learn*
101. Lively & Fun Party Games for Seniors & Elders
102. Role Playing for Sales Champions: From Practice to Performance
103. Fun and Exciting Party Games for Kids
104. Case Studies for Sales
105. Role-Playing for Unbeatable Customer Service
106. Case Studies in Customer Service
107. Case Studies in Winning Negotiations
108. Case Studies in Management & Leadership
109. Case Studies in Human Resources & Talent Management
110. CEO Success Blueprint: The Essential Toolkit for CEOs and C-Level Executives
111. The Salesperson's Self-Coaching Guide: *Master Your Own Self-Coaching Plan for Success*
112. Overcoming Procrastination: *Your Ultimate Guide to Stop Delaying and Start Living Your Best Life*
113. When True Colors Are Exposed: *The Journey to Unmasking Humanity*
114. Life-Changing Habits for Teens: Teen Success Blueprint for a Bright Future
115. Workplace Stress-Free: *Proven Strategies to Thrive at Work and Beyond*
116. Objection Overruled: *The Ultimate Guide to Turning 'No' into 'Yes'"*
117. Building Strong Teams: *A Comprehensive Guide to Team Building*
118. Ethical & Moral Leadership in Business: *Eliminating Unethical Practices & Building a Culture of Trust & Integrity*
119. Rising Strong: Building Positive: High Self-Esteem for a Fulfilling Life-*A Practical Guide for Students, Employees, Leaders & Entrepreneurs*

Besides regularly contributing to business & trade journals, including international ones such as the 'Creative Training Techniques' and the 'Sales News' of the U.S.A, He is also a member of several prestigious bodies & trade associations, having participated in many Conferences & Workshops in India & Overseas.

Prior to his last assignment of leading & managing a large MNC as head, Gerard had a 3-year stint in the Middle East as a Consultant with a leading British Consultancy Firm.

As the past 'Official Country Representative' for the International Business Award- 'THE STEVIES'-(the business world's own Oscar) for about 4 years- he ensured a few Indian companies that qualify for the same every year!

Gerard can be contacted at:

Email: training@Sales-Training.in,training@CollectionSkills.com

Websites:

www.Sales-Training.in
www.EtiquetteWorks.in
www.CollectionSkills.com
www.RetailSalesTraining.in
www.SalesTrainingIndia.com
www.ManualPreparation.com
www.TrainingWithPuppets.com
www.FirstContactAcademy.com
www.SalesAndMarketingRecruiter.com

Our TRAININGS that can help your team

- ✓ **Sales Effectiveness**: Selling Skills for any Sector: Service/ Logistics/ FMCG Realty/ Insurance & Finance/ Media/ SPA's, Health Clubs & Salons/ Key Account Management, Effective Negotiation Skills/ Bid & Proposal Management Skills/ Retail Sales Training: Any Sector (Auto, Jewelry, Clothing, Luxury etc)
- ✓ **Customer Service Skills**-Complaints Handling & Customer Retention
- ✓ **Debt Prevention & Collection Skills**
- ✓ **Etiquette & Grooming**
- ✓ **Leadership & Managerial Skills**
- ✓ **Self & Personal Development Skills**: Presentation Skills/ Effective Communication Skills/Business Proposal Writing Skills/ Problem Solving & Decision Making Skills/ Empowering Secretaries-The perfect PA! (For Secretaries & PA's)/ Effective Time Management/ Teamwork & Teambuilding/ P.R.I.D.E- **P**ersonal **R**esponsibility **I**n **D**elivering **E**xcellence

www.ingramcontent.com/pod-product-compliance
Ingram Content Group UK Ltd.
Pitfield, Milton Keynes, MK11 3LW, UK
UKHW021340190726
13845UKWH00027B/655

9 788198 926289